BEASTS AND THE BATTLEFIELD

BEASTLY ROBOTS AND DRONES
MILITARY TECHNOLOGY INSPIRED BY ANIMALS

Lisa M. Bolt Simons

CAPSTONE PRESS
a capstone imprint

Captivate is published by Capstone Press, an imprint of Capstone.
1710 Roe Crest Drive, North Mankato, Minnesota 56003
www.capstonepub.com

Copyright © 2020 by Capstone. All rights reserved. No part of this publication may be reproduced in whole or in part, or stored in a retrieval system, or transmitted in any form or by any means, electronic, mechanical, photocopying, recording, or otherwise, without written permission of the publisher

Library of Congress Cataloging-in-Publication Data

Names: Simons, Lisa M. B., 1969- author.
Title: Beastly robots and drones : military technology inspired by animals / Lisa M. Bolt Simons. Other titles: Military technology inspired by animals
Description: North Mankato, MN : Capstone Press, [2020] | Series: Beasts and the battlefield | Includes bibliographical references and index. | Audience: Grades 2-3 | Audience: Ages 8-11 | Summary: "Animals have many traits that help them survive in the wild. Inspired by animals' incredible abilities, military forces have created many machines over the years to achieve success on the battlefield. From the first remote-controlled vehicles to the advanced machines of tomorrow, take a look at how military robots and drones often imitate the abilities of animals throughout nature. Then be sure to catch the other amazing titles in the Beasts and the Battlefield series"— Provided by publisher.
Identifiers: LCCN 2019045417 (print) | LCCN 2019045418 (ebook) | ISBN 9781543590210 (hardcover) | ISBN 9781496665911 (paperback) | ISBN 9781543590265 (pdf)
Subjects: LCSH: Military robots—Juvenile literature. | Drone aircraft—Juvenile literature. | Biomimicry—Juvenile literature.
Classification: LCC UG450 .S43 2020 (print) | LCC UG450 (ebook) | DDC 629.8/92—dc23
LC record available at https://lccn.loc.gov/2019045417
LC ebook record available at https://lccn.loc.gov/2019045418

Editorial Credits

Aaron Sautter, editor; Kyle Grenz, designer; Morgan Walters, media researcher; Katy LaVigne, production specialist

Image Credits

Alamy: AB Forces News Collection, bottom 15, 615 collection, 18, Aviation History Collection, top left 13, CPC Collection, top 19, Niday Picture Library, bottom 9, PJF Military Collection, top 7, bottom 20, Science History Images, bottom 26; Associated Press: Christof Stache, bottom 7; Getty Images: John B. Carnett, 22; iStockphoto: danku, (plane) 16-17; Newscom: Dean Murray/DARPA/Cover Images, top 24, Rodrigo Reyes Marin/AFLO, 29; Shutterstock: aapsky, middle 5, Alexia Khruscheva, top 21, Artistdesign29, design element throughout, Bravo_Roger, (hand) left 20, Cathy Keifer, top 9, clarst5, left 16, Creeping Things, (lizard) 10, DarkGeometryStudios, top 28, Dennis Jacobsen, top right 25, Eric Isselee, (skunk) 10, bottom left 25, GJGK Photography, 12, Image Point Fr, 4, In Green, 6, KN2018, top 26, Mark Medcalf, top 15, Martin Mecnarowski, (bird) 17, Martin Voeller, bottom 24, Mirek Kijewski, 23, Nayana Willemyns, bottom 21, Ociacia, bottom 28, Omelchenko, design element throughout, Phillip Rubino, top 5, photosounds, (cat) Cover, reptiles4all, bottom 5, sandyman, (robot) Cover, seeyou, 27, Seregraff, (cat) bottom 13, Suzanne Tucker, bottom 19, Ultraviolet_Photographer, 14; Wikimedia: Denniss, 11,Marshall Astor, middle right 13

All internet sites appearing in back matter were available and accurate when this book was sent to press.

Index

animals, 8, 28
    apes, 20
    bats, 12
    birds, 4, 7, 12, 14, 16, 17, 23, 25
    cats, 13, 19
    dogs, 21
    elephants, 21
    fish, 4
    frogs, 4
    horses, 6, 27
    insects, 10, 21, 22, 27
    monkeys, 20
    mules, 6
    octopuses, 24
    salamanders, 11, 27
    short-horned lizards, 10
    skunks, 10
    snakes, 4

biomimicry, 6

cameras, 12, 16, 19

drones, 6, 14
    Kettering Bug, 8
    Lightning Bug, 12
    MQ-1 Predator, 4
    MQ-9 Reaper, 4
    Pioneer, 7
    Remote Piloted Vehicles (RPVs), 7
    RQ-4A Global Hawk, 17
    RQ-11B Raven, 14
    unmanned aerial vehicles (UAVs), 8, 14, 16
    V-Bat, 25
    Watchkeeper, 16

Ground X-Vehicles, 24

Naval Research Laboratory, 23

robots, 6, 14, 20, 27, 28
    Atlas, 29
    Crocodile Schneider, 8
    Flimmer, 23
    Kobra™, 20
    Legged Squad Support System (LS3), 27
    PackBot®, 20
    Pleurobot, 27
    Ripsaw, 22
    Salamander, 11
    sensor darts, 12
    Shakey, 13
    Small Unmanned Ground Vehicles (SUGVs), 19
    TALON, 20, 21
    Teletanks, 10
    unmanned ground vehicles (UGVs), 6
    uses for
        disarming bombs, 14, 21, 27, 29
        fighting in combat, 4, 6, 8, 10, 11, 22, 29
        reconnaissance missions, 12, 23, 27
        search and rescue missions, 14, 21, 27, 29
        surveillance missions, 17

sensors, 4, 12, 13, 16, 19, 21

wars, 7, 8, 10–11, 12

Read More

Cooke, Tim. *A Timeline of Military Robots and Drones.* North Mankato, MN: Capstone Press, 2018.

LaPierre, Yvette. *How Do Robots Defuse Bombs?* North Mankato, MN: Capstone Press, 2019.

Larson, Kirsten. *Military Robots.* Mankato, MN: Amicus High Interest, 2018.

Noll, Elizabeth. *Military Robots.* Minneapolis: Bellwether Media, 2018.

Internet Sites

10 Surprising Shape-Shifting Organisms
http://listverse.com/2017/11/26/10-surprising-shape-shifting-organisms/

Atlas
https://www.bostondynamics.com/atlas

Flimmer: Flying, Swimming UAV/UUV
https://www.nrl.navy.mil/news/videos/flimmer-flying-swimming-uav-uuv

The Future of Autonomous Robots
https://www.airforce.com/watch-videos/lco1cDHlbEg

Glossary

aerial (AYR-ee-uhl)—relating to something that happens in the air

biomimicry (by-oh-MIM-mih-kree)—imitating the design of a living thing

engineer (en-juh-NEER)—someone trained to design or build machines, vehicles, bridges, and other structures

humanoid (HYOO-muh-noid)—shaped somewhat like a human

infrared (in-fruh-RED)—invisible waves of light that are usually given off by heat

radar (RAY-dar)—a device that uses radio waves to track the location of objects

reconnaissance (ree-KAH-nuh-suhnss)—gathering of information about an enemy

surveillance (suhr-VAY-luhnss)—keeping close watch on someone, someplace, or something

terrorist (TER-uhr-ist)—someone who uses violence and threats to frighten people

torpedo (tor-PEE-doh)—a type of missile that usually travels underwater

ultraviolet (uhl-truh-VYE-uh-lit)—invisible waves of light that can cause sunburn

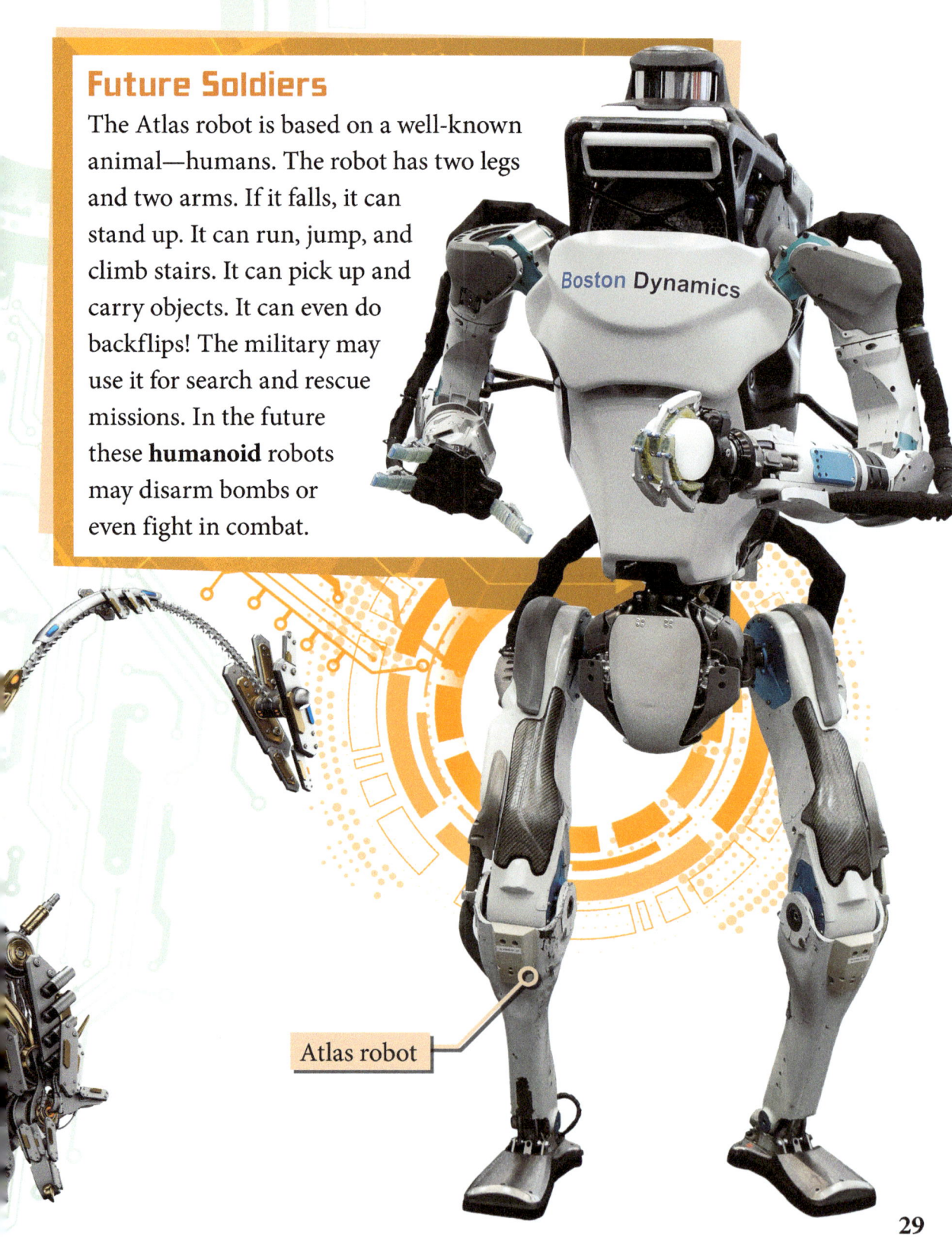

Future Soldiers

The Atlas robot is based on a well-known animal—humans. The robot has two legs and two arms. If it falls, it can stand up. It can run, jump, and climb stairs. It can pick up and carry objects. It can even do backflips! The military may use it for search and rescue missions. In the future these **humanoid** robots may disarm bombs or even fight in combat.

Atlas robot

An artist's idea of a future drone

Time Will Tell

Animals have developed unique features to survive in the wild. Inventors and engineers often study animals to build better machines. Studying animal abilities has led to many useful robots. Following nature's example, these machines can help keep soldiers safe on future battlefields.

An artist's idea of a future robot

Copycats

Some robots look like the animals they are based on. The Legged Squad Support System, or LS3, is like a robotic horse. It can carry about 400 pounds (181 kg) for 20 miles (32 km). These robots may one day help troops carry heavy gear across battlefields.

The Pleurobot looks like a salamander's skeleton. It's about the size of the Japanese giant salamander. It can walk over bumpy ground. It can also swim. The robot may someday help in search and rescue missions.

FACT
Engineers are also designing robots that move like cockroaches. These small robots will have six moving legs and joints. They could help gather information, disarm bombs, or find land mines.

The LS3 robot can carry heavy gear over rough land like a horse.

Researchers hope to create machines that change shape while flying. Inventors will have to study animals like the northern white-faced owl. When facing a threat, the owl changes its shape to look more frightening.

The northern white-faced owl can change its shape to scare off enemies.

FACT
The V-Bat drone can fly straight up like a helicopter. Once in the air, it can soar like a bird. It flies well in windy weather. It can fly quietly for about eight hours.

25

Ground X-Vehicle wheels can change into a triangle shape.

Flexible Features

Inventors are also working on Ground X-Vehicles. These machines have wheels that can change shape based on the land. Some animals, like the octopus, can also change themselves. They change their color and shape based on their surroundings.

An octopus changes its color and shape to hide among the rocks.

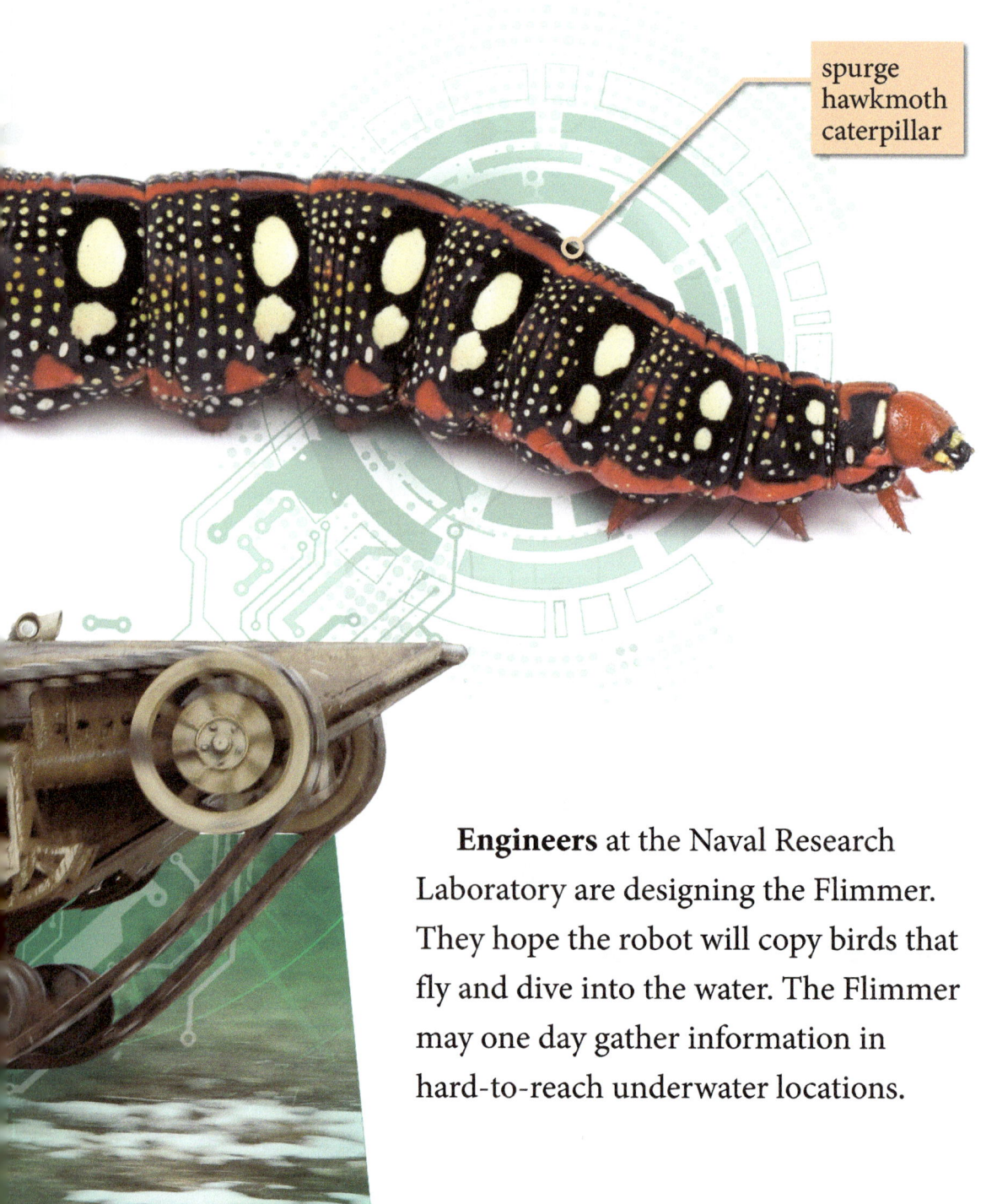

spurge hawkmoth caterpillar

Engineers at the Naval Research Laboratory are designing the Flimmer. They hope the robot will copy birds that fly and dive into the water. The Flimmer may one day gather information in hard-to-reach underwater locations.

Missions of the Future

Inventors keep looking to nature to create new designs. The Ripsaw is a high-speed tank. Its tracked wheels work like a caterpillar's legs. The machine easily climbs steep hills. It smoothly rolls over obstacles. U.S. forces hope to use the unmanned robot tank in future combat.

Ripsaw tank

These robots are often used to disarm bombs. They also perform dangerous search and rescue missions. They even imitate a dog's sense of smell. Their sensors can detect dangerous chemicals in the air.

TALON's sensors act like a dog's sense of smell.

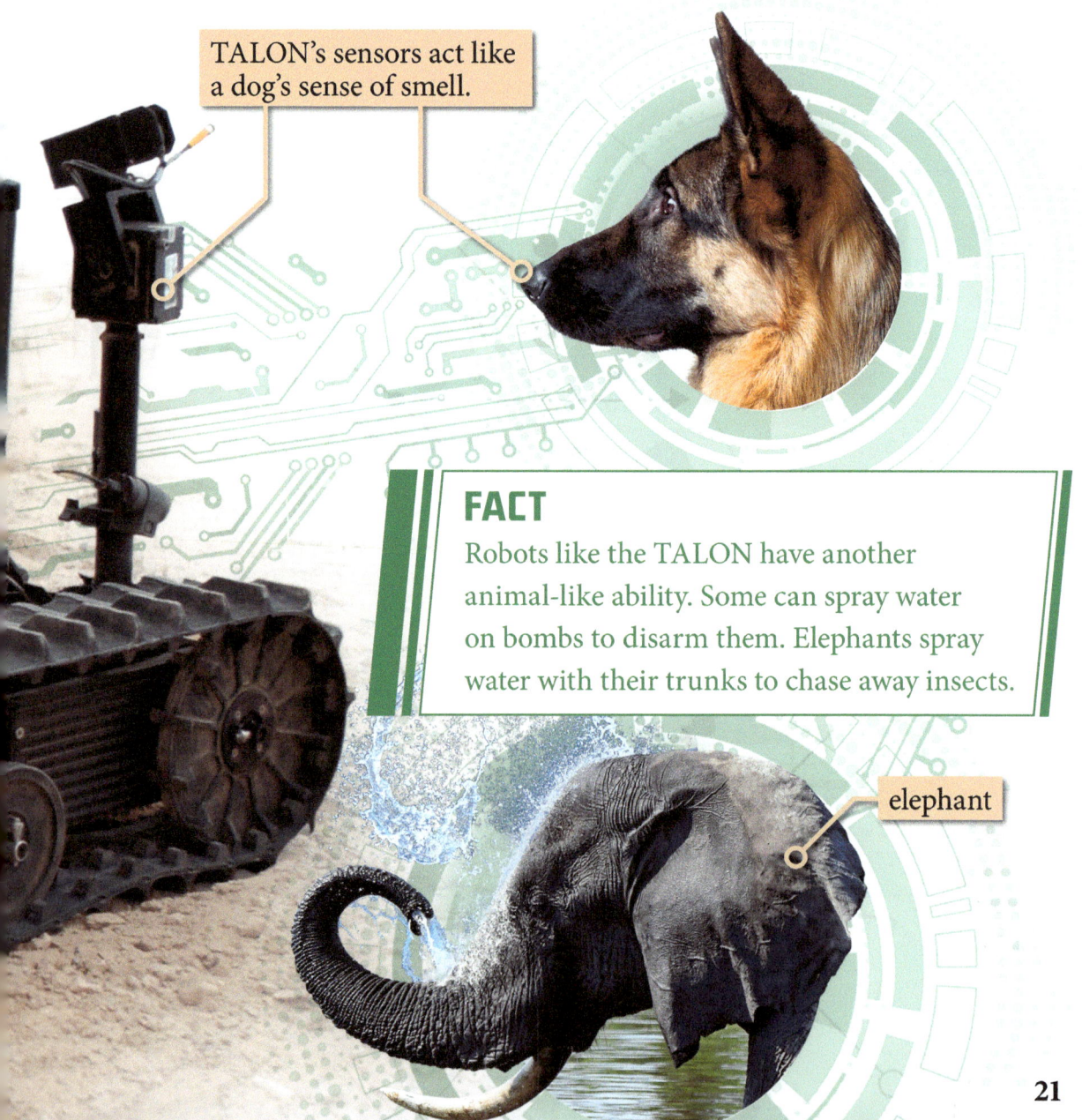

FACT
Robots like the TALON have another animal-like ability. Some can spray water on bombs to disarm them. Elephants spray water with their trunks to chase away insects.

elephant

Climbing, Grabbing, Lifting, Smelling

The PackBot®, TALON, and Kobra™ are all similar robots. They travel over uneven ground with tracked wheels. They climb stairs as easily as mountain goats. The robots can also pick up objects. Their grippers work like the hands of monkeys and apes. The Kobra's™ arm can lift up to 330 pounds (150 kg).

TALON's gripper works like a monkey's hand.

SUGV

Robot Toss

Soldiers often need to make sure buildings are safe. To do so, they sometimes use Small Unmanned Ground Vehicles (SUGVs). They toss the 5-pound (2.3-kilogram) robots through windows. If one lands on its back, it can right itself like a cat. The robots have other catlike features. They have cameras and sensors for great sight and hearing. They quietly search buildings for danger.

Light-weight SUGVs can be carried into action.

condor

The condor is a large bird that flies well in strong winds. It soars through the air with its wide wings. The RQ-4A Global Hawk performs **surveillance** missions. Like the condor, the Global Hawk is a strong flier. It can fly even in bad weather.

RQ-4A Global Hawk

goldcrest bird

Soaring and Searching the Skies

The goldcrest bird is only 3.5 inches (9 cm) long. It's small, but it's a great flier. It can fly more than 300 miles (483 km) without stopping. Some UAVs also make long nonstop flights. The British Watchkeeper can fly for 16 hours straight. Its **radar**, camera, and sensors gather information about enemy locations.

kestrel

A soldier prepares to launch a RQ-11B Raven.

Animal-Inspired Protectors

Modern machines often copy animal features too. Military robots and drones help find enemies and disarm bombs. Some help in search and rescue missions. Just like animals, these machines come in all shapes and sizes.

Infrared and **ultraviolet** (UV) light are invisible to humans. Kestrels hunt prey using UV light. The RQ-11B Raven is a small UAV. It hunts out targets like kestrels hunt for prey. But the Raven uses infrared light instead. It can find people in the dark.

A flower under UV light

The Lightning Bug's cameras acted like a hawk's sharp eyes.

FACT

In the 1960s researchers built a robot named Shakey. It shook as it moved. The robot had sensors like a cat's whiskers. The sensors could detect objects. Shakey used its sensors to find a path around objects.

Shakey's sensors acted like a cat's whiskers.

Eyes and Ears in Vietnam

Drones were important in the Vietnam War (1954–1975). The Lightning Bug was often used for **reconnaissance**. The drone hunted for enemies like an eagle or hawk. It had powerful cameras. The drone could see enemies from thousands of feet in the air.

U.S. forces also created long darts with giant sensors. The sensors acted like a bat's super sense of hearing. Soldiers threw the darts from airplanes. The darts landed in thick jungles and listened for enemies. Information about the enemy's location was then sent to U.S. forces.

Some machines were designed to make surprise attacks. The U.S. Navy created the Salamander in 1944. The unmanned craft crawled from the water to blow up enemy defenses. Like real salamanders, it could travel both in the water and on land.

Soviet TT-26 remotely controlled Teletank

Natural Offenses

Skunks and stink bugs can spray chemicals from their bodies. The short-horned lizard can squirt blood from its eyes! Animals use this ability for self-defense. Armies found this feature useful too.

In World War II (1939–1945) the Soviet Union invented the Teletank. Like some animals, the remote-controlled tank could spray enemies. It could shoot smoke, fire, or chemicals.

skunk

short-horned lizard

The Kettering Bug flew like a fluttering moth or butterfly.

Past Inventions Lead to a Robotic Future

The natural world is dangerous. Animals have abilities that help them survive. Battlefields are also deadly. To keep soldiers safe, researchers often look to nature. They create machines that imitate animal features.

Armies began building unmanned vehicles in World War I (1914–1918). French forces created the Crocodile Schneider. This small tracked machine crawled like a crocodile. It blew up when it reached its target.

U.S. armed forces tried making unmanned **aerial** vehicles (UAVs) too. The Kettering Bug was like a **torpedo** with wings. After a set amount of time, the engine shut off. The craft would then drop like a bomb to hit its target. But the war ended before the Bug was ready for combat.

Pioneer unmanned aerial vehicle

Mules and unmanned ground vehicles can carry heavy loads.

Robotic Capture

The Gulf War took place from 1990 to 1991. The U.S. armed forces used many Remote Piloted Vehicles, or RPVs, in the war. Pioneer drones reminded enemy troops of soaring vultures. One group of Iraqi soldiers surrendered to a Pioneer. Five men waved white flags at the drone. It was the first time enemy fighters surrendered to a flying robot.

Imitating Nature

Military ground robots are called unmanned ground vehicles, or UGVs. Like mules or horses, these robots carry supplies on the battlefield. They also help carry injured fighters to safety.

Many robots and drones are designed to imitate animals. This process is called **biomimicry**. *Bio* means "life." *Mimesis* means "to imitate." Drones and robots often do dangerous jobs that humans can't. Some experts believe these machines are the future of the military. By 2025 or 2030, robots may outnumber troops in combat.

MQ-9 Reapers soar on wide wings and spot distant targets just like eagles.

Both snakes and MQ-9s use infrared light to find targets.

Robo-Warriors and the Natural World

An unmanned aircraft called the MQ-9 Reaper streaked across the sky like an attacking eagle. The target was the **terrorist** group ISIS. The United States military battled this group in 2016. Enemy fighters tested the soldiers' skills. The armed forces fought back with unmanned aircraft. The Reaper and the MQ-1 Predator made many perfect strikes. They caused little damage and spared innocent lives.

The MQ-1 and MQ-9 used special sensors. They worked like some animals' eyes. Some snakes, frogs, and fish can see **infrared** light. Animals use this light to help locate prey. The MQ-1 also used it to locate targets.

infrared image

Table of Contents

Robo-Warriors and the Natural World 4

Past Inventions Lead to a Robotic Future 8

Animal-Inspired Protectors 14

Missions of the Future 22

Glossary 30
Read More 31
Internet Sites 31
Index 32

Words in **bold** are in the glossary.